Broken Beautifully

A poetic tale of falling into madness and finding the courage to claim myself

Stephanie Carroll

Second Edition

Publishing/ copyright page

Published by Stephanie Carroll

Cover design by Stephanie Carroll

Cover photo by Alayna Dawson

Photography by Alayna Dawson

Edited by Sara Jean-Phillipe

Edited Second Edition by Delores Stuart

Second Edition, 2022

ISBN: 978-1-7368309-1-8

Note to Reader

Dear Beautiful Reader,

First of all, thank you for picking up this book. The words in this book have been in my heart to share with the world. I have always felt compelled to share my life in writing. That inspiration has taken many forms and transformations to arrive at this debut. I hope this poetic collection you have found provides you with whatever you need it to. We all have stories, and my passion is to find the beauty in all of our stories. Allow yourself to enter into mine and allow the journey to be what you need.

Broken Beautifully

Stephanie Carroll

Contents

Part I: *Lulled*

Fell into you, into your lure

Enamored by illusions, enthralled into the fairytales

Contents

Part II: *Vile*

Enwrapped with disgraceful touch

Part III: *Poisoned*

Poured violent words into my skin

Ambiguous demeanor kept me confound

Contents

Part IV: *Enchanted*

Hid within castle walls made of steel

Reckless abandon allowed me to feel

Part V: *Gifts*

Contradictory sweet lies & scary truths

Emerged resilient courage & vivid inspiration

Contents

Broken Beautifully

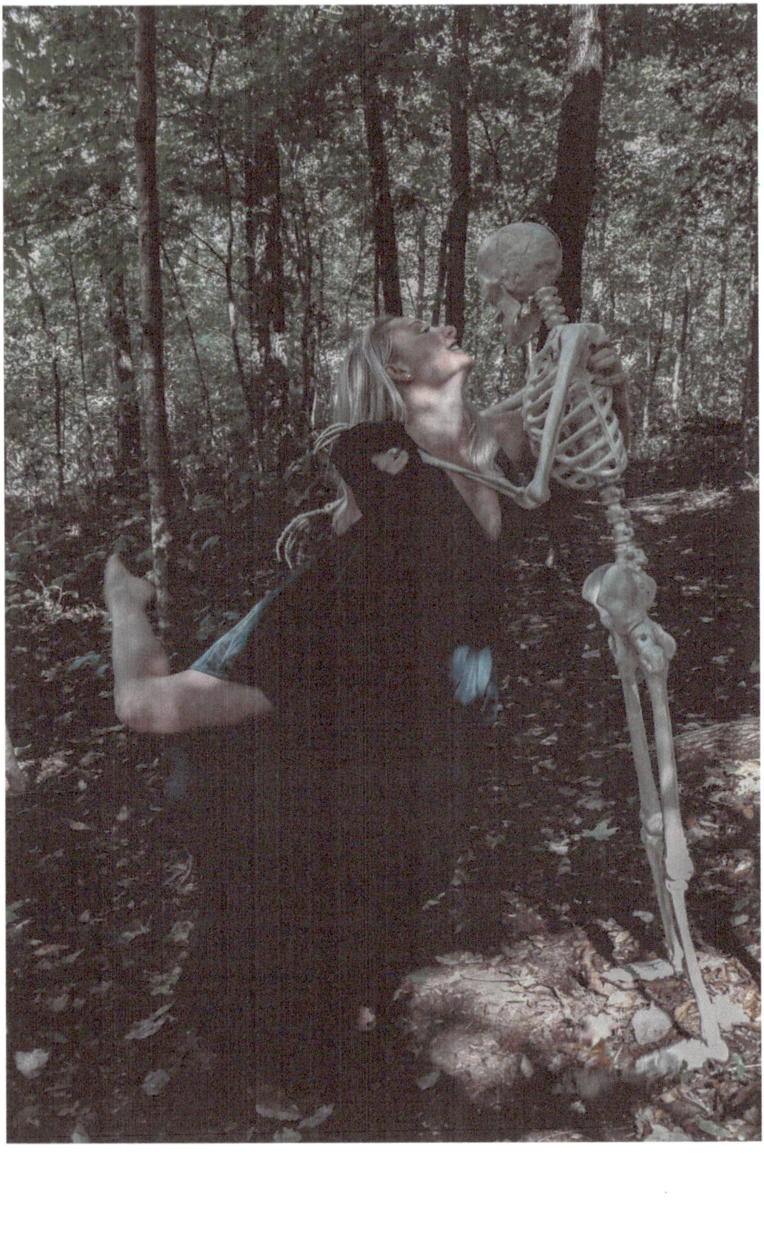

Lulled

I felt things.
Made dangerous seem safe,
dreams erode into nightmares.

-Dangerous

I cry because I realize
he never loved me
Such a beautiful lie
he told himself

He confused my imperfections
with his lack of willingness
to bend for me

He told me I was safe
asked me to reveal
my secrets
to him

Then

My secrets
were used against me
to bury me
to abandon me
he knew exactly
how to ruin me
and ruin me
he
a l m o s t
did

-Ruin

Sold me the nightmare disguised as my dream

-Disguised

It only
happened once.
But it played a
thousand times
in my mind.
I found it
in the look
of his eyes.
It came to me
in every decision.
Agonizing
over the right choice.
So that day
may never
find me
again.

-Once

Pry inside my mind
Expose my weakness

Plan your torments
Make me afraid

Raise your voice
Abandon me in shame

Possess me like a doll
Drown out my words

Count your conquests
Dismiss my worth

Throw your blades
Open my scars

Collapse on top
Own my flesh

Salvage my pieces
After the crash

Rehearse your charm
Drive me insane

-Rehearse

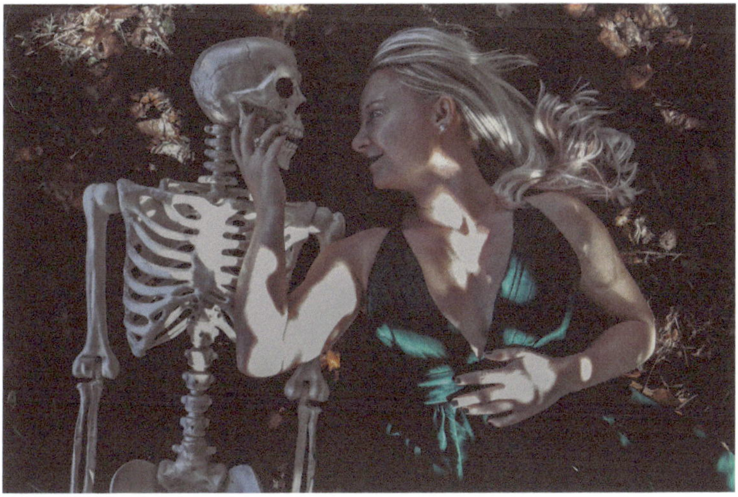

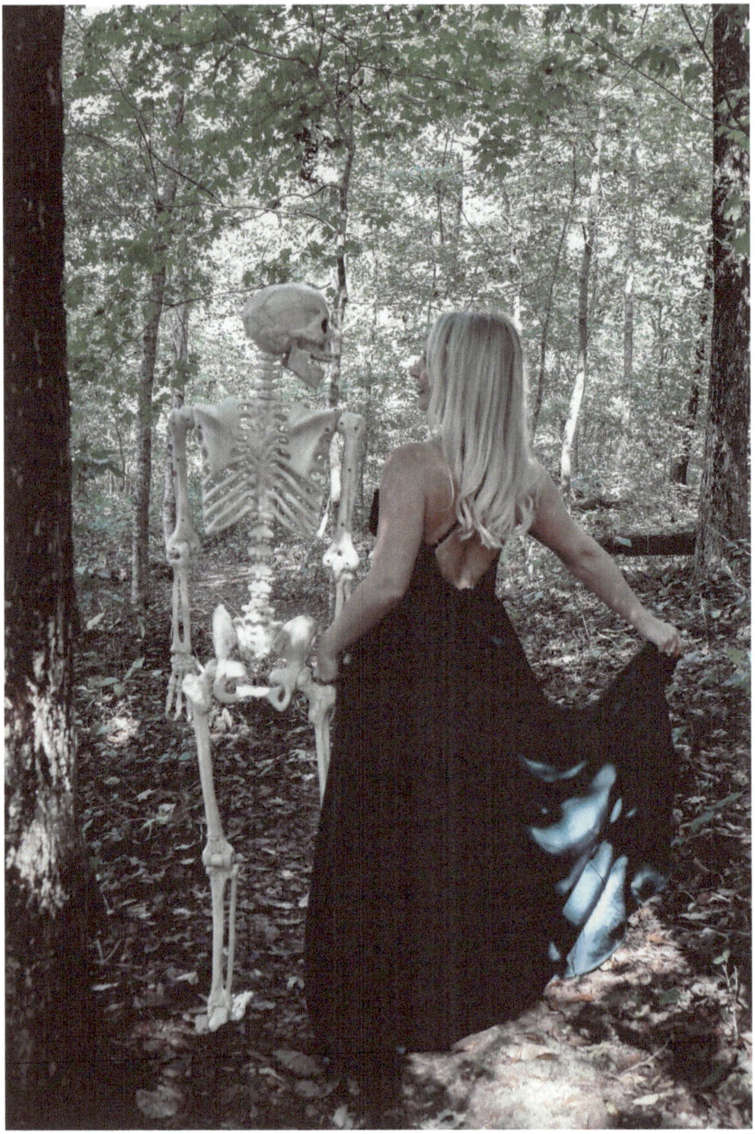

Your bottles

are full

of my broken heart

and soul

smashed together.

-Smashed

The clock ticks with thoughts of you
Sometimes fast. Other times slow
One hour closer to when you come home

Nighttime comes so quick
My body works so hard to digest you
Always a different flavor I will be forced to swallow

In the beginning, the flavor was sweet
A taste I never knew existed. Made me addicted
Flavors are illusions
That tasty toxin. That perfect poison
Formulated to keep in a delusion
The kind that tell lies
The kind that get me choosing the lies

Those days when the cloud bank lowered
Clouds coated in fairy dust
I am still. So still.
You have moved the clouds for me
An illusion of me being higher. Happy
That sweetness and human side that drew me in
I raped my own mind
How do I make this scene stay
Impossible hoops. Out of reach jumps
If I bury my needs further. If I give up my purpose
It will stay this way. This beautiful day

And then. Inevitably. Abruptly. Here comes the storm
The clouds race back up to the sky
I see the picture so clearly now
The misery that is my truth if I stay
Most days, I say lie to me

-Lie

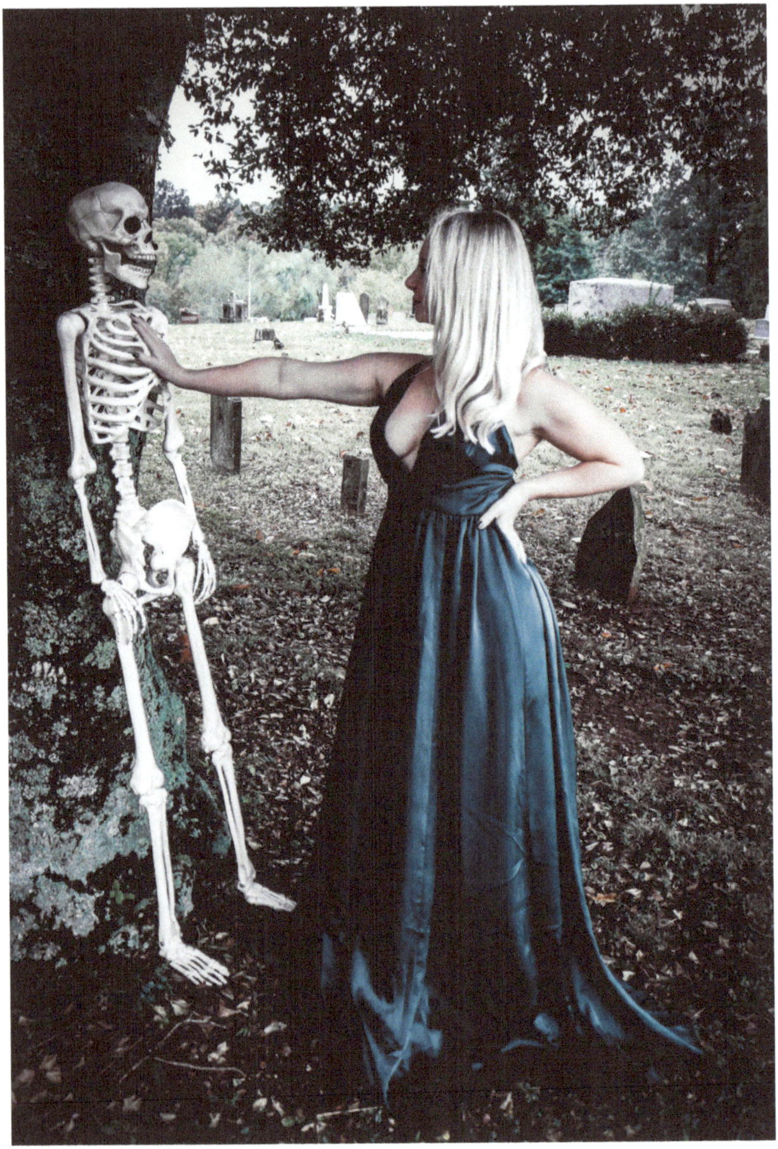

Vile

My peace was stolen from me

but now I wonder if I ever knew peace

Maybe that's how you infected me

-Infected

Scream your fabrications at me
with such conviction
that I wonder if I'm wrong
I lived my life,
but do you know it
better than me?

Condemn me for your lies on me
when the same truth
gives you such power
a man playing make-believe

Skin hums, thoughts race
trying to hold onto anything tangible
to find the strength that you're wrong

-Scream

My body wasn't my body anymore
you degraded it, debased it

I confused your chaos for conviction
I thought you were choosing me
I was just an idol to you. An idea
A representation

I wasn't human to you
I was skin to debase, giving you control
I was a brain to drive insane, increasing your power

My words were saved and twisted for your pleasure
My body was degraded for your perversion
My mind was turned inside out trying to survive you

-Degraded

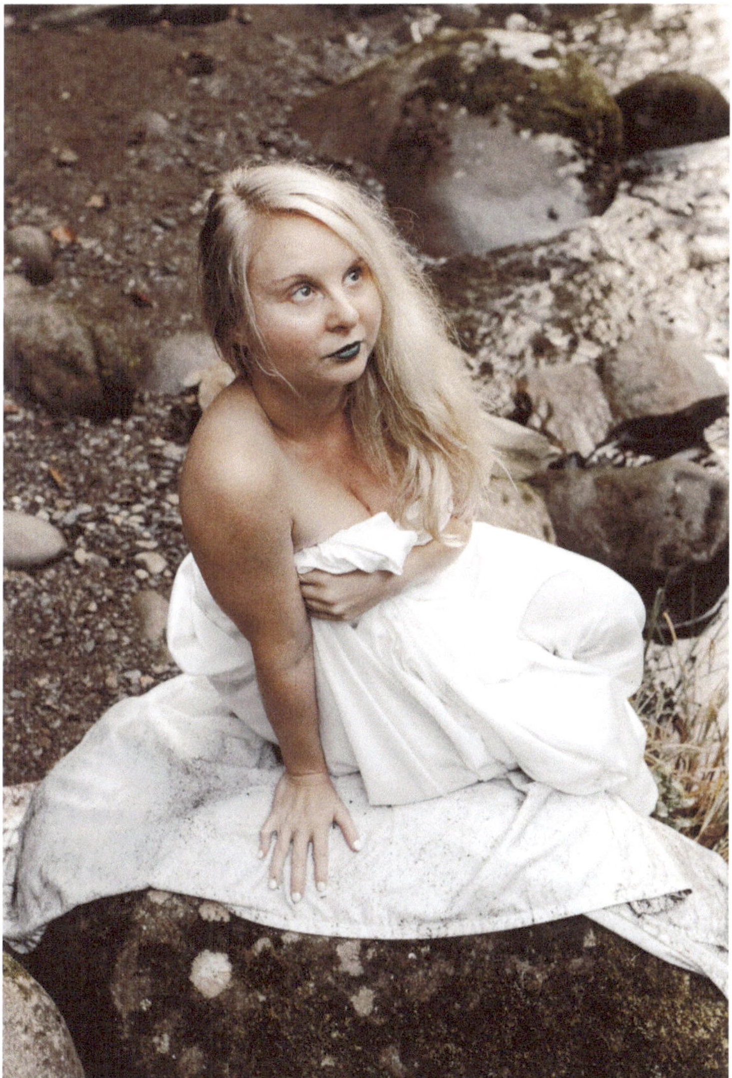

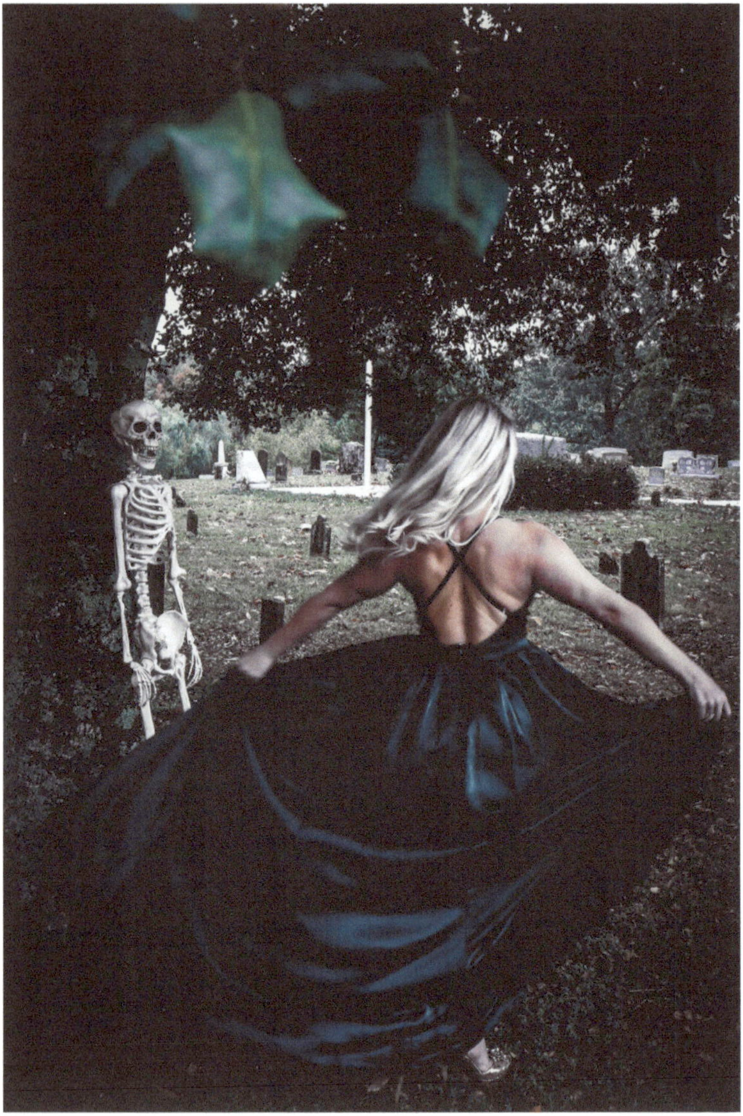

Are you even human?
Charming but rehearsed
Caring but controlling
Fabricated safety to poison

Made me question my sanity
That my body even belonged to me
Every time you entered me
You betrayed me
In a thousand ways

So subtle
So oblivious to you
So insignificant
Something to be owned
Poisoned my body
Devalued my worth
Damaged me beyond recognition

If you ever had a soul, you sold it
If you ever had a heart, you cut it out
And now
There is only evil where humanity should be

-Human

What a vile creature you are. Do you know
Body riddled with invisible scars

Do you know what you did
Defiled my innocent skin

Sucked me into your decrepit world
Where the ceilings are the floors

A l m o s t   to the edge of I can't take any more

Smeared your ghostly poison, like sheer daggers
contaminated my light

Spoke curses with your tongue
Bound them with your love

-Creature

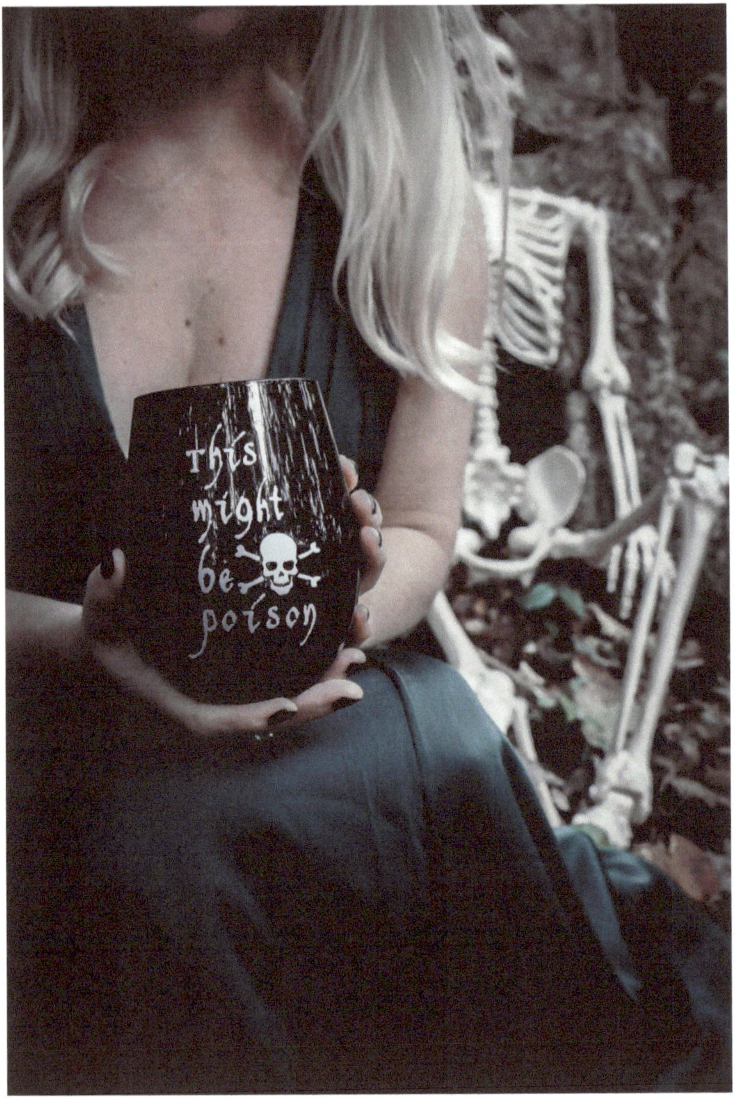
this
might
be
poison

Poisoned

People
stain
your
life
and
it's
never
the
same

-Stained

My veins run black
With your poison
You were my drug
When I needed it the most
Watching someone die slowly
In front of me
You were my drug to survive
Then your poison ran red
With danger
To my body, mind, & soul
Walls turned to steel
Blood turned ice blue
Frozen to survive you

-Frozen

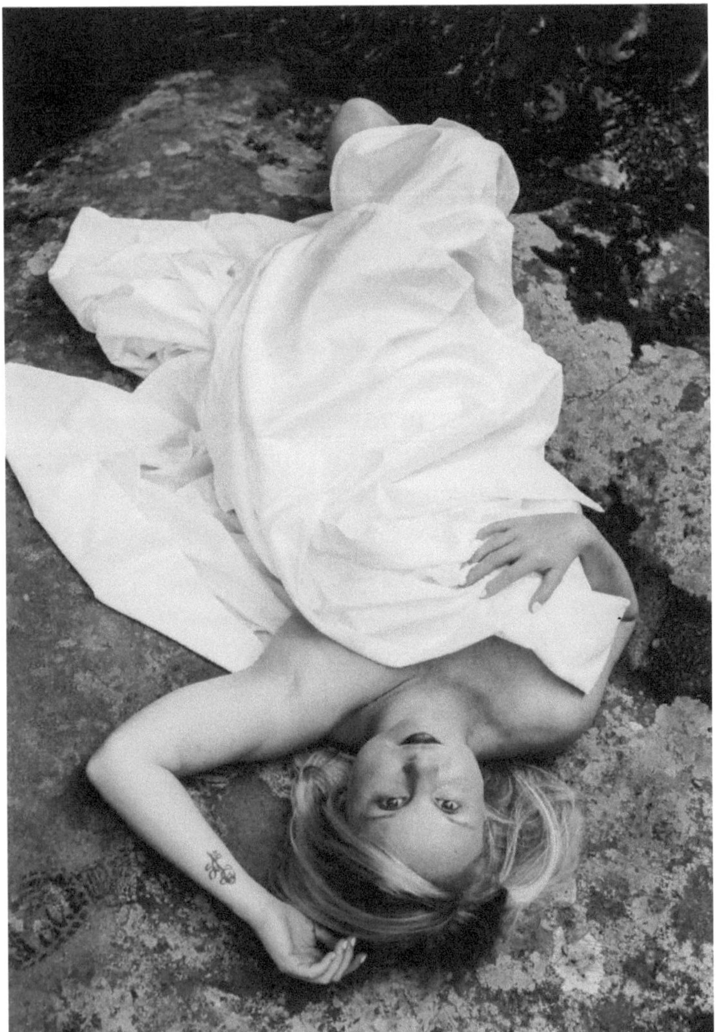

Became
a
living
dead
body

Just
to
keep
breathing

-Dead

Suddenly
it covered me
Surged through me
I knew
your strength
would be no match
for mine.

As scared
of you as I was
I was more scared
of me
And what I could choose
to do to
escape you

-Escape

On the last day
I say my absolute truth.
Every word I held back
I say it with such dominance.
I scare him.
I step into my worth.
Gathering my things.
My clothes.
My dignity. My sweetness.
I stand up with my items and walk.
Away.
To. Never. Return. Ever.

-Gather

I’m free from you now.

In my veins

In my blood

I’m trapped.

I’m

still

trapped.

-Trapped

You made me

bleed

my soul

trying

to save yours

-Bleed

You tried to bury me
Suffocate me with your toxin
Gaslight me with your lies
Light me up
Illuminate me
Encircle me
Until I have you surrounded

All the pain, I turn into power
Your pain becomes my grace

-Grace

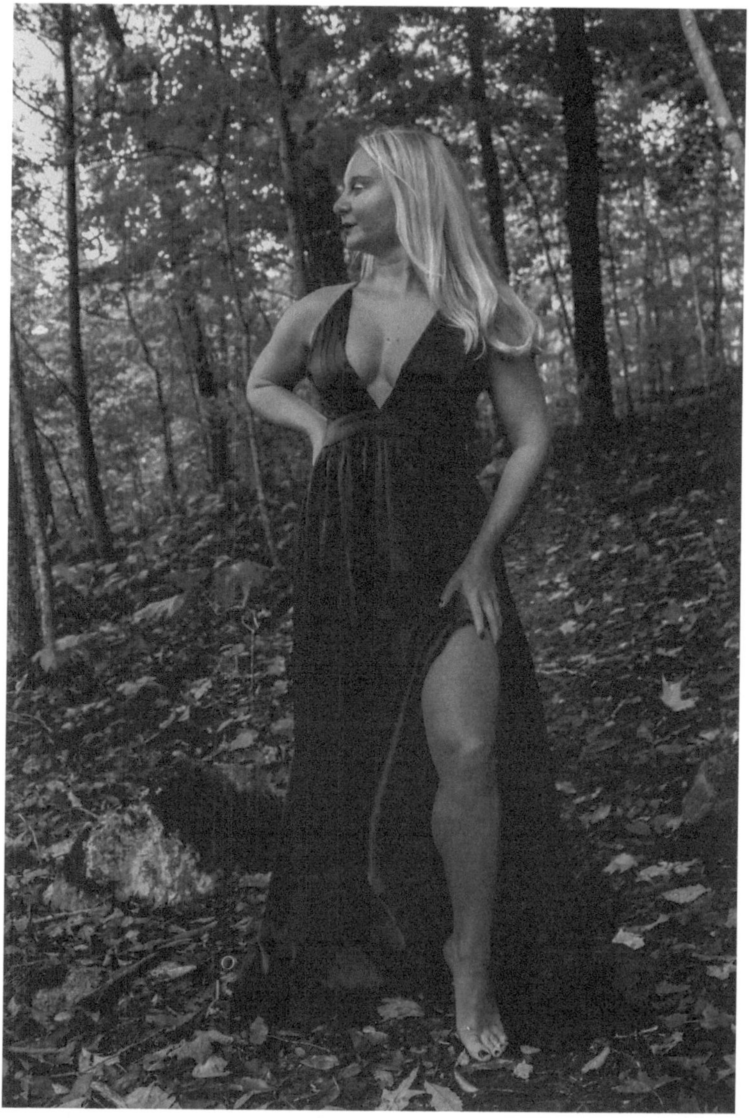

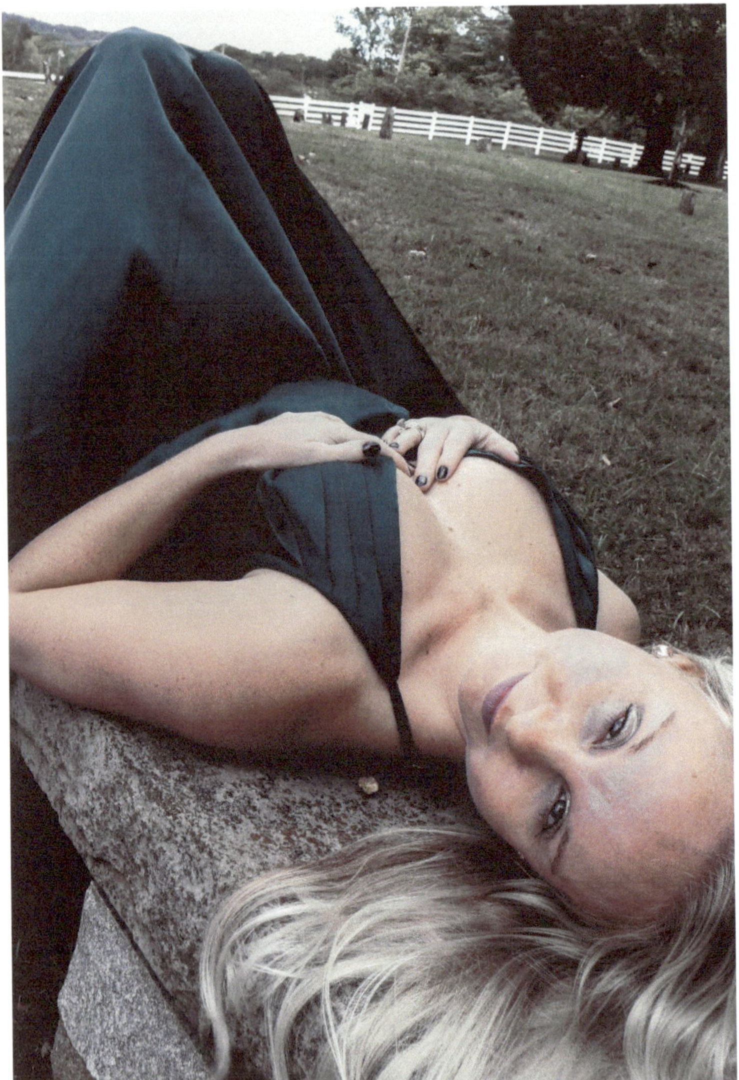

Enchanted

I'm a witch
put your terrors in my
cauldron
Let me brew my
potion
Brew it
just for you
I'll take everything you
threw
Black as night
emerged
luscious green
Abundance & Love
adorned for a
queen

-Brewed

Vile tongue kept you high & me drained
Heavy hips kept me chained

Mirrored eyes got me lost, drew me in
Perverse words, liquid over my skin

Defiling hands, cruel mouth
Enwrapped me in scars, told my secrets

All your haunting, penetrating parts, I release
For forgiveness for myself and peace for you

All of your haunting vicious parts
Now, my ingredients, revive my heart

Inside my cauldron, I brewed my spell
Transformed night into pastel

-Pastel

I’ve seen you haunting me
Not wanting to let me go
I never faltered after I left you
You will never touch me again
Never again did I cry over you
Never again did I miss your touch

-Touch

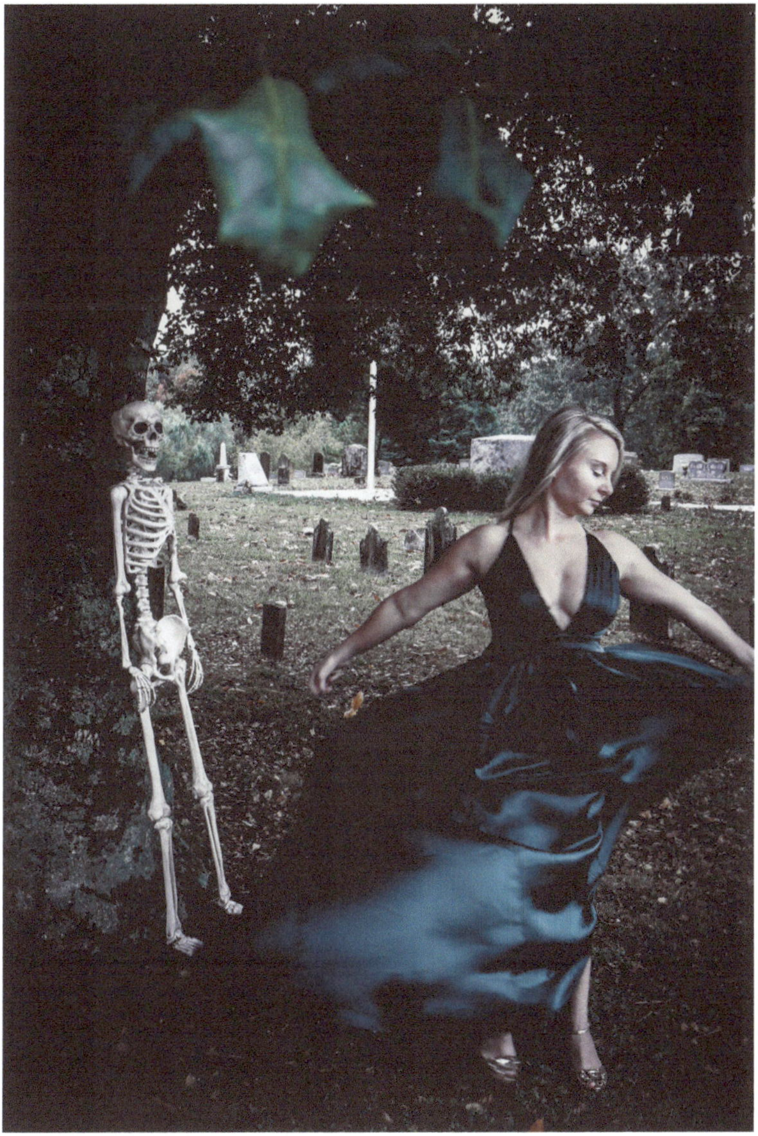

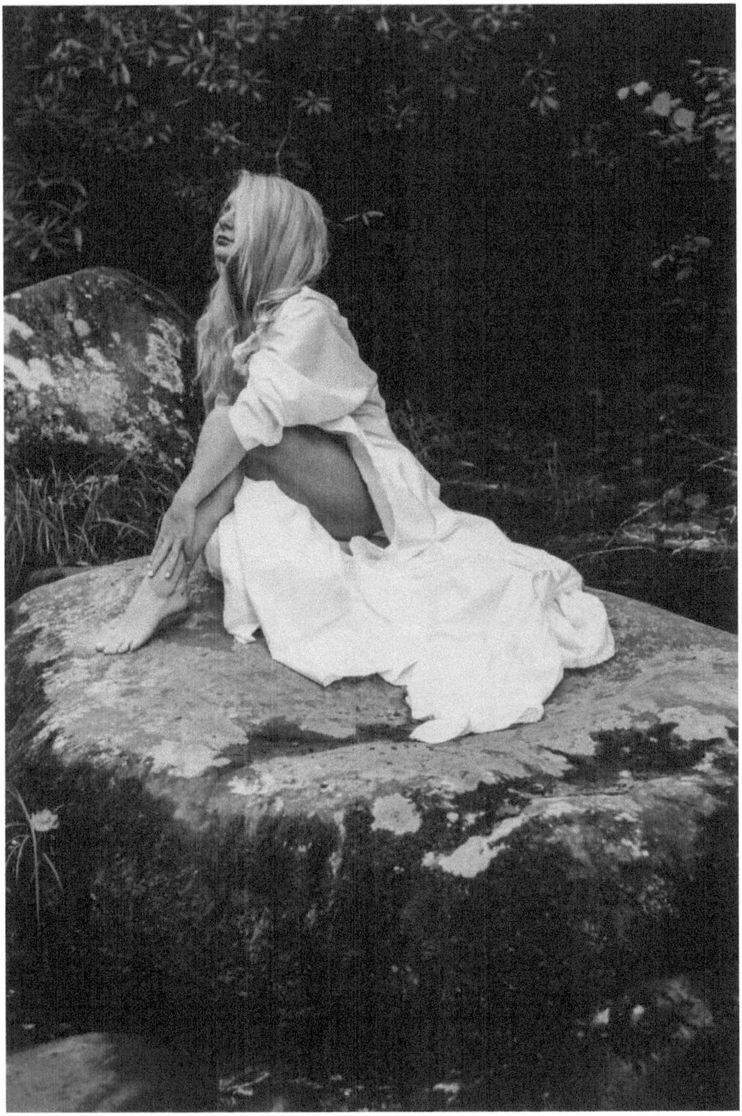

Shatter your eyes using your vision for pain
Bound your body the way you kept me chained

Run your mind through a maze cold and demented
Feed you fabricated salvation to keep you beaten

Stab your heart with daggers laced with venom
Mouth running black choking on poison

Take all your infectious behavior and reverse
Conjure a wrath explicitly tailored and observe

Watch your fiction unravel and regress
Take back my life, you no longer possess

Revenge would only keep your demons circling me
I choose to be free

What I choose to do
Is live in a world where your hate only consumes you

Vengeance is me leaving you the way you were found
Forgiveness is peace. A sweet, serene sound.

-Serene

Hating you
only fuels the poison
And I release
your poison back to you
I feel sorry for you
only for a moment
only a moment was spent
wishing you well
from this day forward,
I only think of me
and the tranquility
I am closer to finding

-Release

I won't cast spells on you
I only cast spells to be free of you
I take back my power that you held captive
You built a cage made of glass,
but I am made of steel

Freedom is now my only will
Freedom from you. Freedom from my past
Freedom from the darkness that built my path to you

I've uprooted all the poison
And plant my path with roses
Strong and soft
A symbol of my beauty that you never touched
Beauty that you only released

You were my rude awakening
I will not thank you
It was not because of you
It was inside me all along

All your torment and rage in fear of my love
Hurry, make me insane before I realize
the light inside of you was only a reflection of mine
Hurry step on my ambition before
my ambition takes me through the door

I did not close the door, watch me walk
Oh no. I will not look back and miss you
I have the strength to walk away with you buried
in the house you've made
I have the strength to walk away, leaving you
exactly the way I found you

-Found

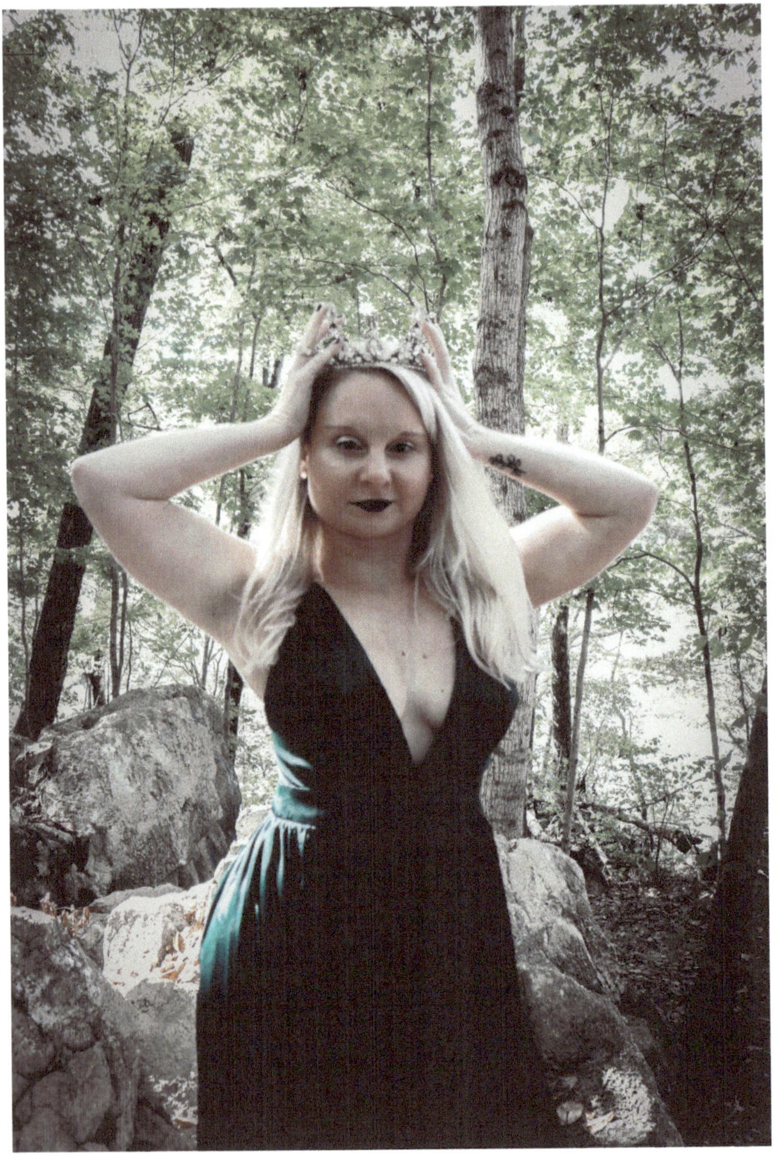

Gifts

I am reclaiming myself

from you

You didn't really break me

Did you?

But, how you tried

-Reclaim

What did you SEE
My heart pumping for those around me

What did you TAKE
My soul longing to be seen

What did you FIND
Yourself basking in my warm light

What did you SUFFOCATE
My mesmerizing, reviving glow

Formulated the scheme, executed the ruse

Someone to console me from
My SADNESS

Save me from
Cruel INJUSTICES

But you missed something
Something eluded your malice mind

I SEE
My courageous DEFIANCE

I TAKE
My unshakable STRENGTH

I FIND
My unbridled essence

I BREATHE new life into me
Give back the nightmare disguised as my dream

-Give

Sweet, lovely gifts
buy me pretty things when
you think are you buying me
controlling me

Sick, loathly gifts
attempts to make me complacent
in the war you rage against me

oh, sweet narcissist
how you've deceived yourself

I took your darkness, your key
and opened my own door
door to my demon world
facing yours, I wasn't scared of mine

Oh sweet narcissist, no wonder
you were scared
face to face with a woman
with the courage to see her truth and yours

What a gift you gave me

-Key

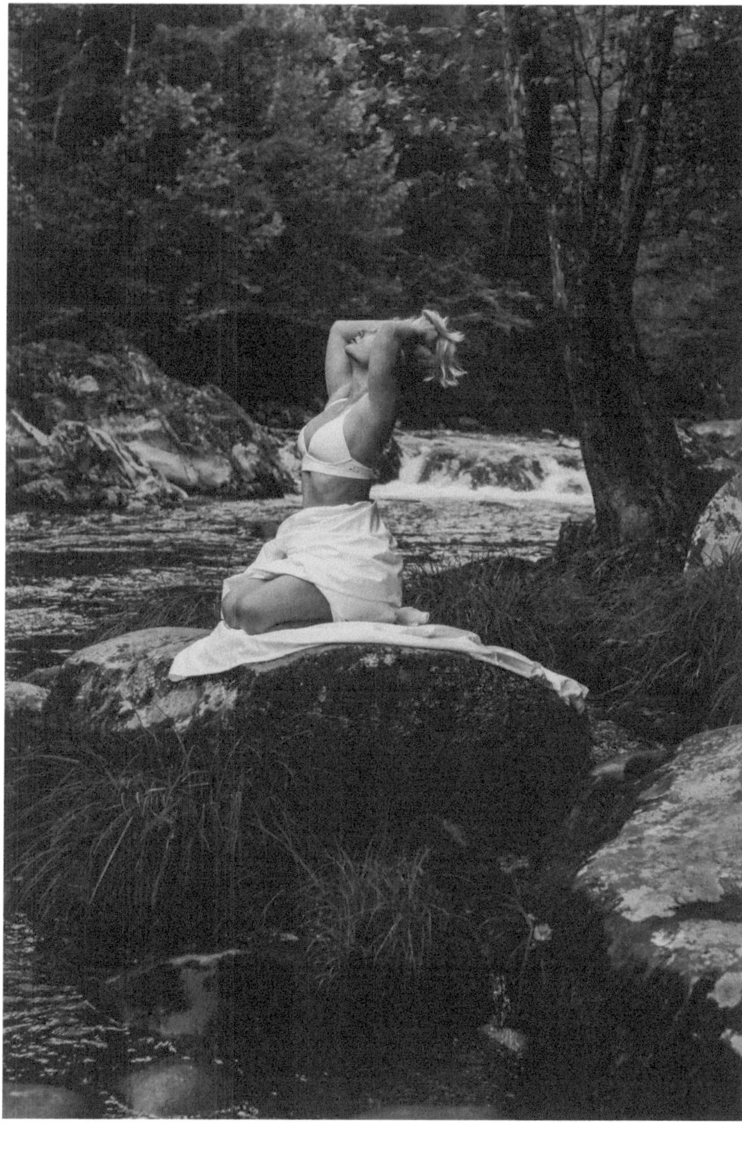

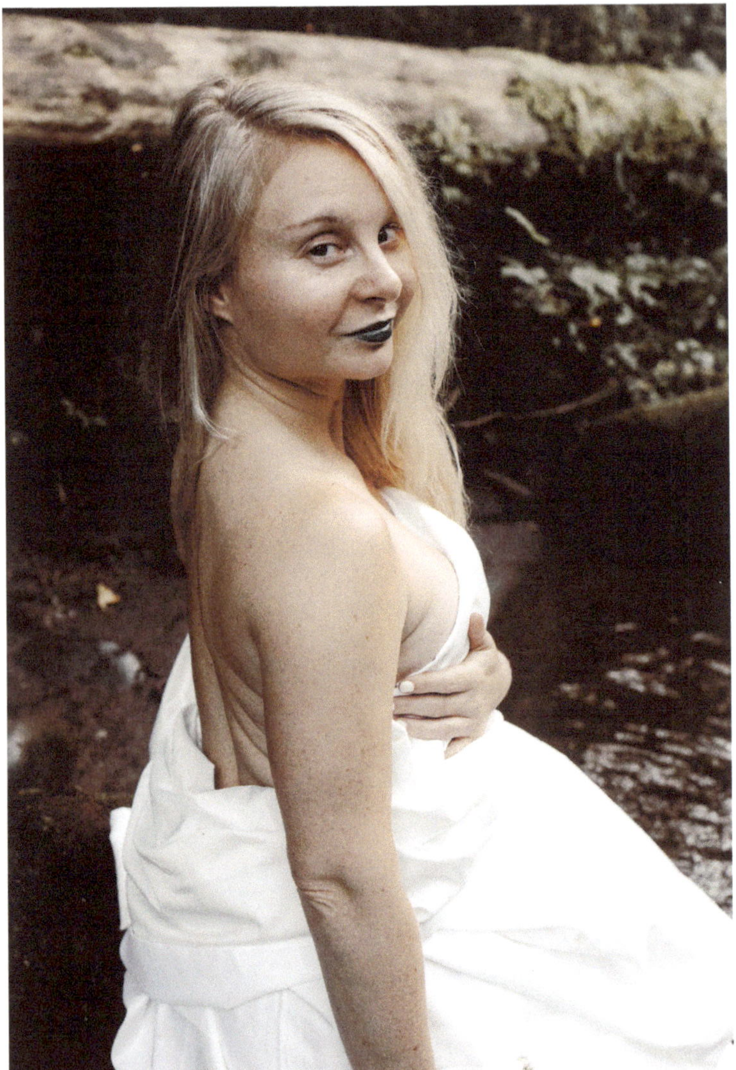

Narcissists are made

Narcissists make you

-You

Not realizing that I was already buried
You crashed your darkness on top of me

Buried since infancy
You brought me to life

I found myself in your torment
Ignited my strength to breathe
To live

You brought me a storm
I learned how to command it

Let the rain pour down on me
Wash every ounce of you away

Lightening cracks your lies
Tornado rips me from your hold
Wind floats me to safety
Flood drowns your restrains
Fire consumes you to ash

-Storm

you are ashes
my soul is amber
my heart ignited the fire

I am water
calm at the shore
raging on the horizon

you are the ashes
I am the waves
erasing your touch

I am the light
eradicating your words
forgiving your smile

-Erase

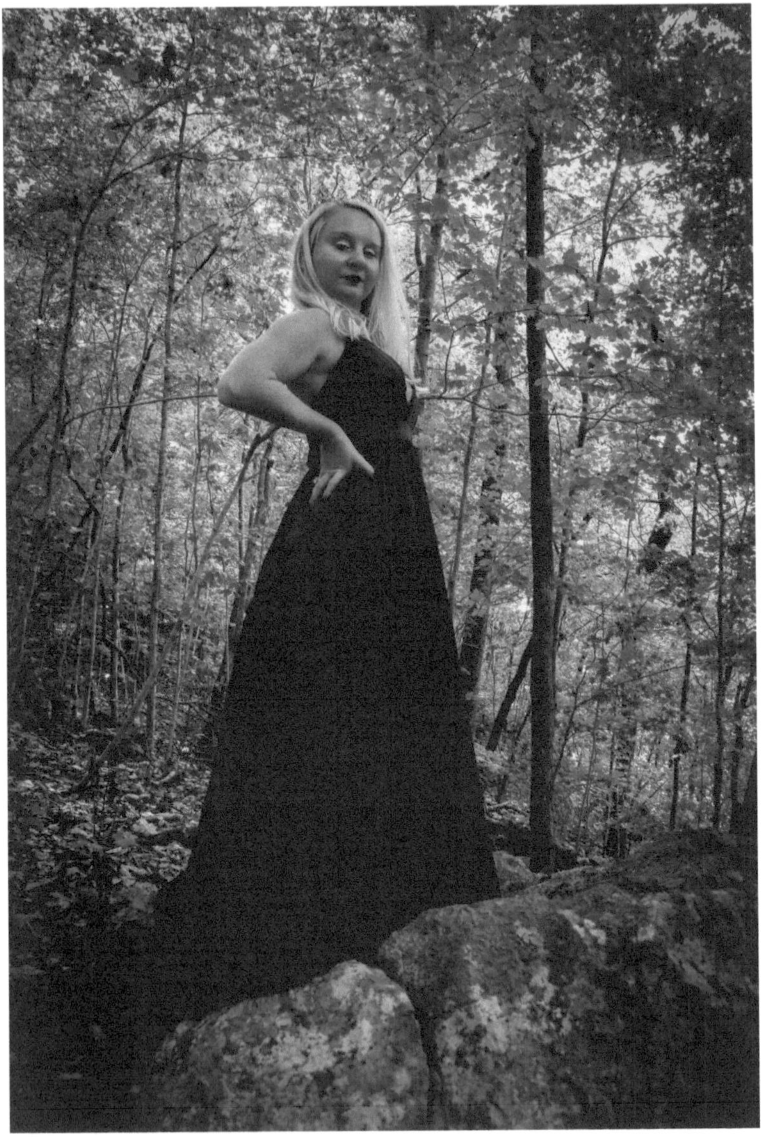

Refusing to bow to a Queen
your envy turned to emerald green
Haunted you are by Her crown
you are running lost, She is standing found

Your light was stolen by your ghosts
Which person scares a narcissist the most

Oh, lonely stealer
No match for a Healer
you are a devil, she is Divine
Her tears transform into wine

-Bow

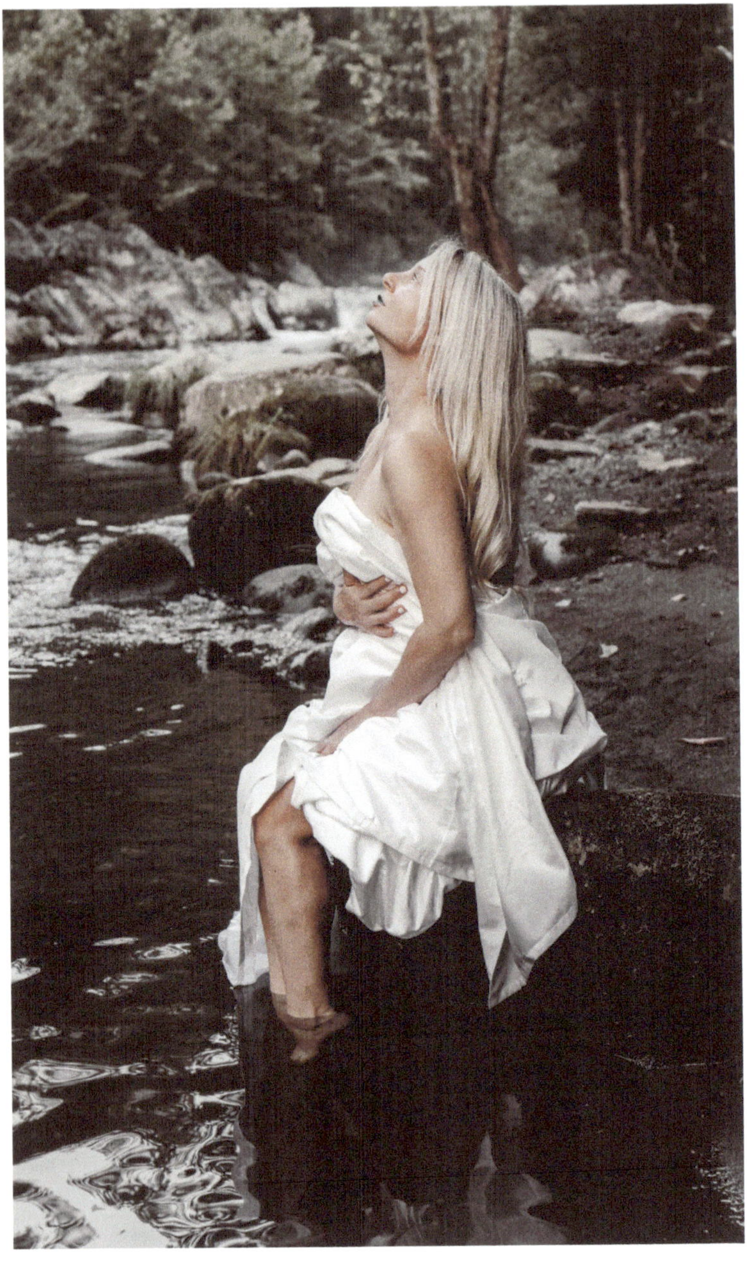

Heal

Delicate
footsteps

led to you

Fierce

leaps

bring me to myself

-Fierce

Ghostly emotions held deep

Banish you from my body

Every single piece reclaimed, revived

-Banish

With my soul ignited after surviving you,
I will harness my power to dive deep
heal the wounds that allowed
me to fall into your world

-Harness

I see you in my mind now
you are farther away
sometimes I feel compelled
to remember you
my brain, my body worked tirelessly
to forget you, almost entirely
remember you just enough
to keep me safe
I dream of a world
where I will no longer be tied to you
not remembering you with fear
just as someone I once knew
It wasn't all bad, it wasn't all torture
this is what made us even worse
the magic entwined around the demons
the demons of your soul
trying to provoke the demons of mine
I believe you did take pleasure in my pain
I could blame you irrevocably
I take responsibility for running
right into your insanity with open arms
a little boy playing at being a man
a lost little girl scared of being a woman
let all the masks fall to the floor
let us both be seen for who we truly are

-Masks

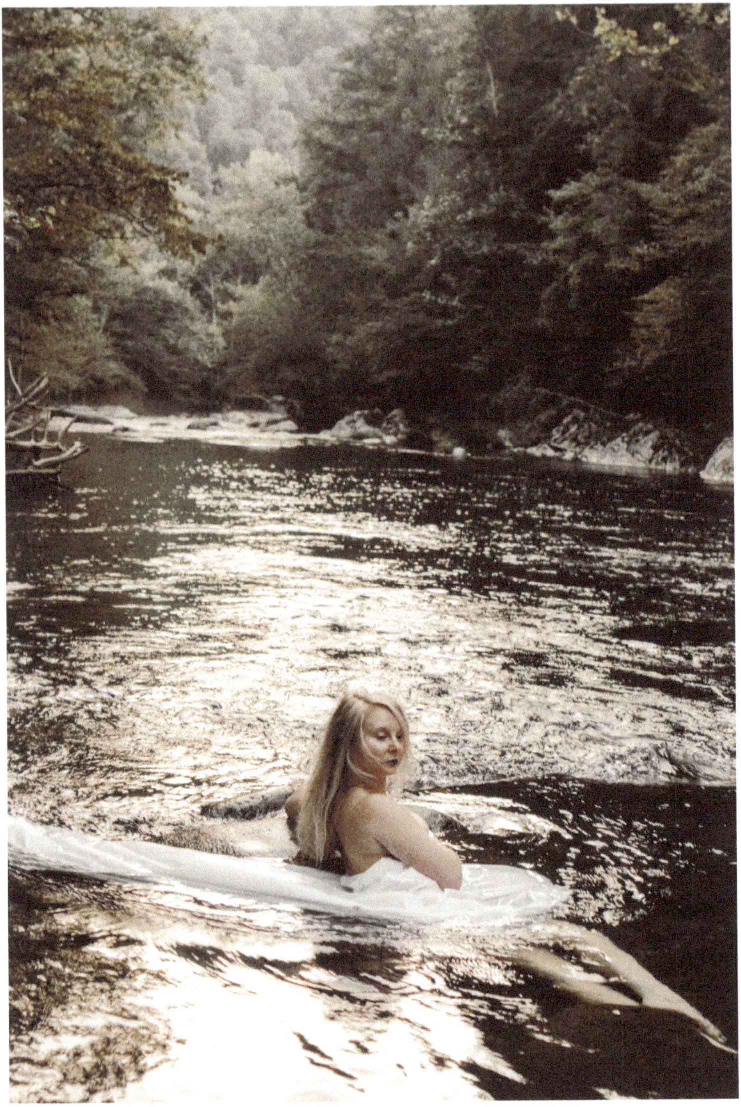

Water washes you away
and brings me back to myself

-Water

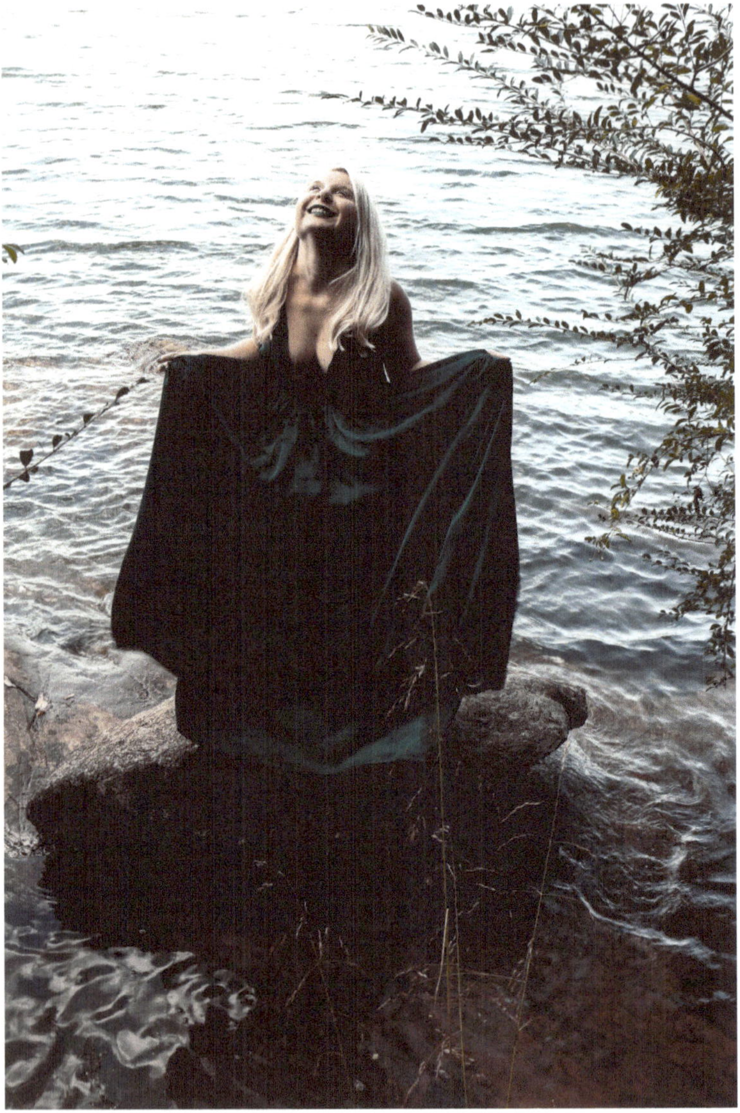

So in love

with the memory

of being free

from you

-Free

I watched him crash
into my truth like I did his
His truth was vile.
Counting. Conditional.
My truth is love.
Full of grace. Lively.
Realizing how my truth was more powerful than his.
How maybe he knew all along.
Worked so hard to lie to me.
Narcissists are scared. Truly scared.
Those of us with beauty in our hearts
and strength that doesn't run away.
Strength that even runs toward that lost soul
who we mistook for a human.
What strength that is.
Narcissists need that strength.
We are their drug.
And at one time they were ours.
The difference is
the narcissist is just as lost as before.
We come out braver. Wiser.
Shattered and in need of healing.
But now on the changed course,
a journey to transformation.
The narcissist is the warning sign of unhealed trauma
and the opportunity for true healing to begin.
What darkness I saw. What magic I see now.

-Truth

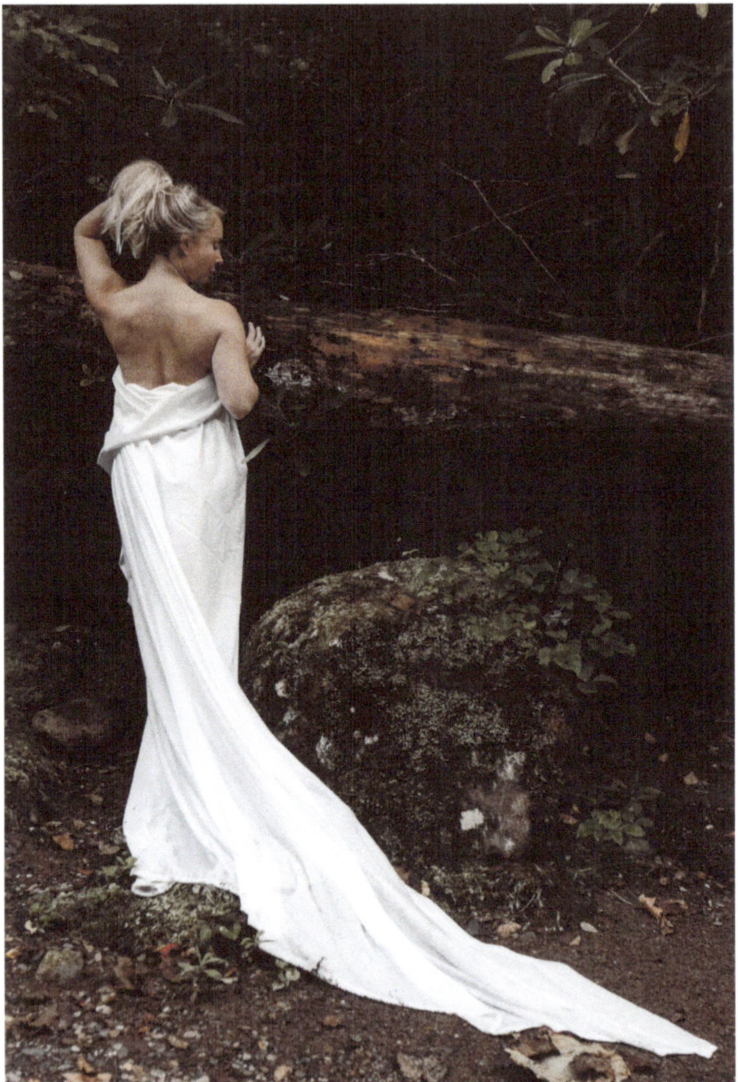

The events of my life left me wanting to be saved. And he found me. It didn't take long to fall into the whirlwind of his admiration for me. I'd never had someone pursue me so intensely, treating me like a queen. I thought this must be true love. After the love bombing, it started slow, with strange twisted comments entwined with the charming person I had met. Soon, I fell into the madness and I started to question my own mind. His accusations were shouted with such conviction, and the mind games were absolutely mystifying. Eventually, I started researching signs of abusive relationships on the internet every day to hold on to my sanity. I wasn't ready to let him go because he was my drug to handle the other part of my life that fell into tragedy at the time. Leaving him just seemed too much to handle. So I told myself I can be better, I can make him be kind to me, I can make him see the way he is treating me is wrong. It took me a year to say out loud to him that he was abusive. His response, "Yeah I can be." It would be 10 more months before I would start packing my bags and this time I didn't stop. After I left that night, I never returned. It wasn't until I stumbled across a self-help course for survivors of narcissistic abuse that I would realize what I went through was actually narcissistic abuse and understand the level of damage it had inflicted in my mind, body, and heart. And that I was primed to fall for him because I had not healed the trauma before him. Two years after leaving him, I begin trauma therapy and began an art journal of my healing journey. Now I feel compelled to share my words and my story through photography and poetry.

Acknowledgments

Blushed Moments Photography

Alayna Dawson

Thank you so much
for capturing this journey with me.
It's always a pleasure working with you.
Your soul radiates authenticity and
I love all of our shoots together.

Find Alayna's work on Instagram
@blushedmomentsphotography

Acknowledgments

Sara Jean-Philippe

So much of my professional growth
and the progress of this book
has come from inspiration solely
from you, my beautiful friend.
You inspired me to put photography
and poetry together and I'm truly proud
of the work I have created.
Your advice has allowed this passion
project to fall into a place
where I feel ready to bring it into the world.
So grateful to know you.

Find Sara's Poetry on Instagram
@sincerelysj

Acknowledgments

For those of you, you know who you are, that
helped me along this journey in any way,
Thank You So Much.

If you read my book and
gave me feedback, Thank you.

If you encouraged me, Thank you.

If you helped me on this journey by following
me into the darkness and sitting with me
there, while I brought healing into my heart,
and found the words to describe it, Thank you.

All of your gifts have played a part in me
bringing life into this gift.

I honor you and I'm proud to know you

About the Author

Stephanie Carroll is a dreamer, aerialist, self-healer, and survivor. After finding herself in the same patterns with different people, again and again, reliving her deep childhood wounds, she embarked on her healing journey. Stephanie's journey began over three years ago. She has documented the experience from the very beginning in an art journal as she courageously dove into her wounds that came with adoption and the fear to be truly seen.

Stephanie writes from a place where she invites you into the deepest parts of her soul, touched by abandonment, adoption, emotional neglect, grief, domestic emotional abuse, and the war within her. Trying to make sense of it all, she truly finds herself as she releases what no longer serves her.

Stephanie has first-hand experience of what it takes to heal the mind, body, heart, and soul from a lifetime of adversity. She has trained in an array of healing modalities including earning a master's degree in Mental Health Counseling from Carson Newman University. Stephanie is passionate about healing and inspiring others on their healing journey.

www.ingramcontent.com/pod-product-compliance
Ingram Content Group UK Ltd.
Pitfield, Milton Keynes, MK11 3LW, UK
UKHW061026310726
14090UKWH00024B/418

9781736830918